1 | Big Farm

Name
Date 6-9-16

To parents Have your child trace the path with his or her finger, then with a pencil. For extra practice, have your child continue to trace the path with different colored pencils. Give your child plenty of encouragement and praise.

Draw a line from the arrow (➡) to the star (★) by following the path.

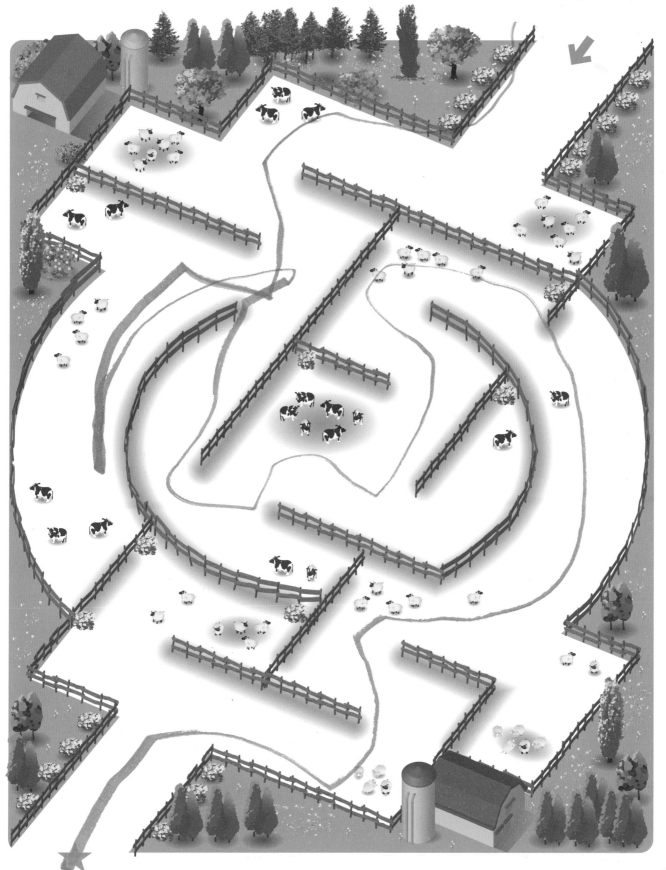

Draw a line from the arrow (→) to the star (★) by following the path.

2 Fresh Vegetables

Name	Gavin
Date	6-9-16

Draw a line from the arrow (→) to the star (★) by following the path.

3

Draw a line from the arrow (➡)
to the star (★) by following the path.

Courtyard Castle

Name Gavin

Date 6-9-10

Draw a line from the arrow (➡) to the star (★) by following the path.

5

Draw a line from the arrow (➡) to the star (★) by following the path.

4 **Under the Sea**

Name
Gavin

Date
6 - 9 - 16

Draw a line from the arrow (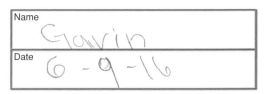) to the star (★) by following the path.

Draw a line from the arrow (→) to the star (★) by following the path.

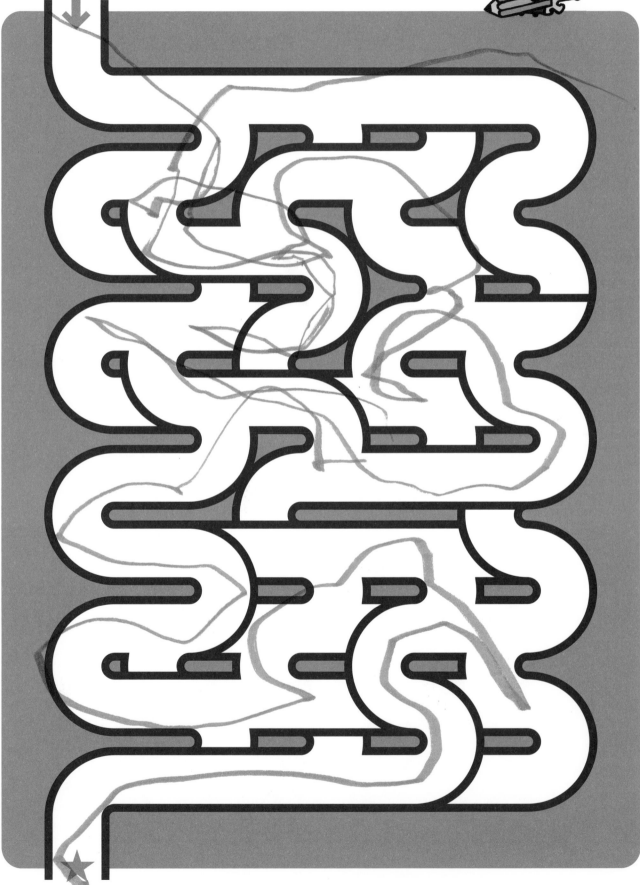

8

Name Gavin
Date 6-9-16

Draw a line from the arrow () to the star (★) by following the path.

9

Draw a line from the arrow () to the star (★) by following the path.

Name Gavin
Date 6-9-16

Draw a line from the arrow (➡) to the star (★) by following the path.

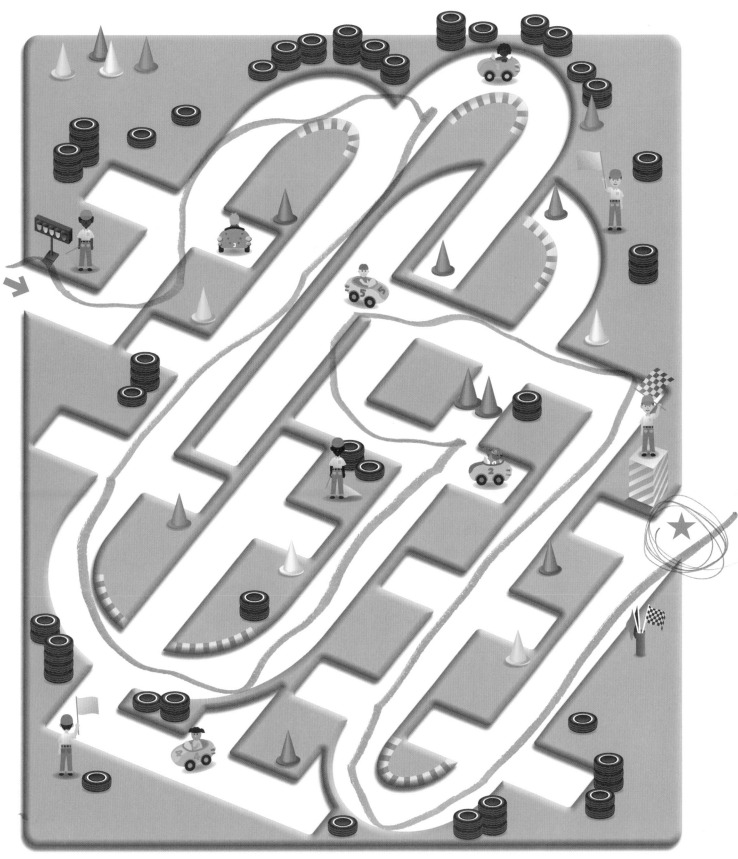

Draw a line from the arrow (→) to the star (★)
by following the path.

Autumn in the Park

Name Gavin
Date 6-9-16

Draw a line from the arrow () to the star (★) by following the path.

13

Draw a line from the arrow (→) to the star (★) by following the path.

Touring the Town

Name Gavin

Date 6-9-16

Draw a line from the arrow () to the star (★) by following the path.

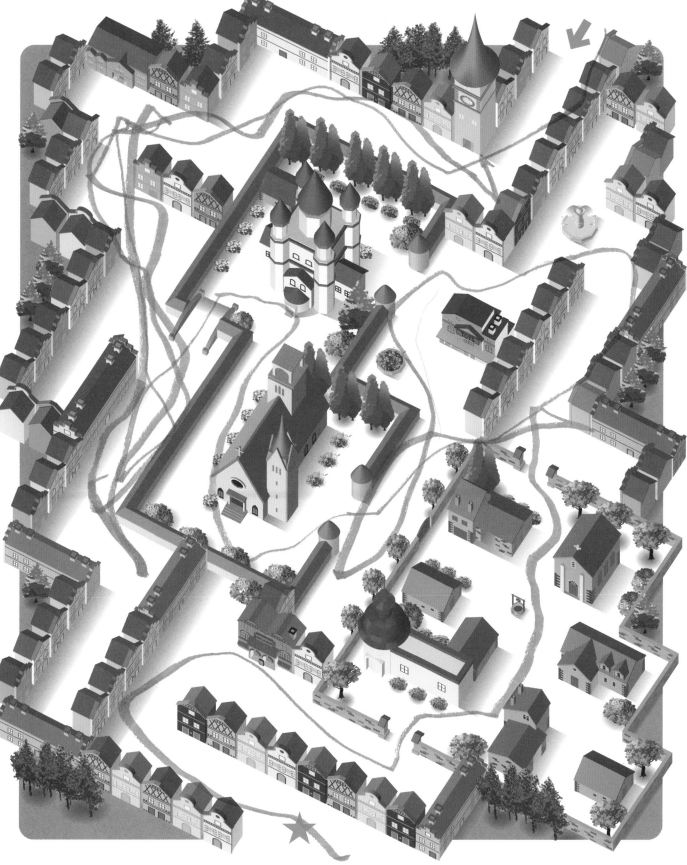

Draw a line from the arrow (➡) to the star (★)
by following the path.

Name Gavin

Date 6 – 9 – 16

Draw a line from the arrow () to the star (★) by following the path.

Draw a line from the arrow (→) to the star (★) by following the path.

10 Garden Courtyard

Name Gavin
Date 6-9-14

33 seconds

Draw a line from the arrow (➡) to the star (★) by following the path.

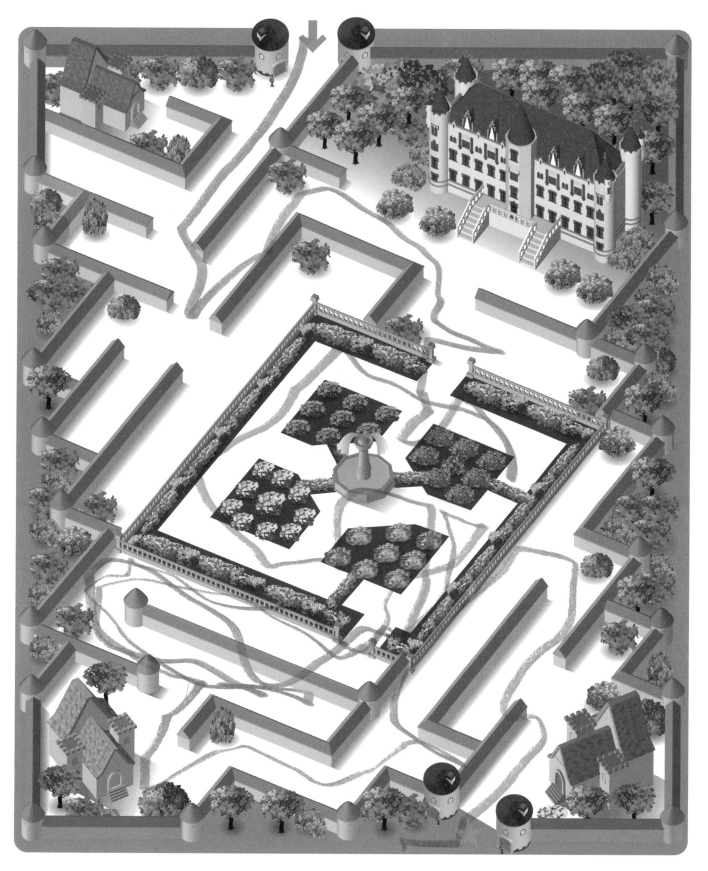

19

Draw a line from the arrow (➡)
to the star (★) by following the path.

30 seconds

20

11 Where Is My House?

Name Gavin

Date 6-9-16

20 seconds

Draw a line from the arrow (→) to the star (★) by following the path.

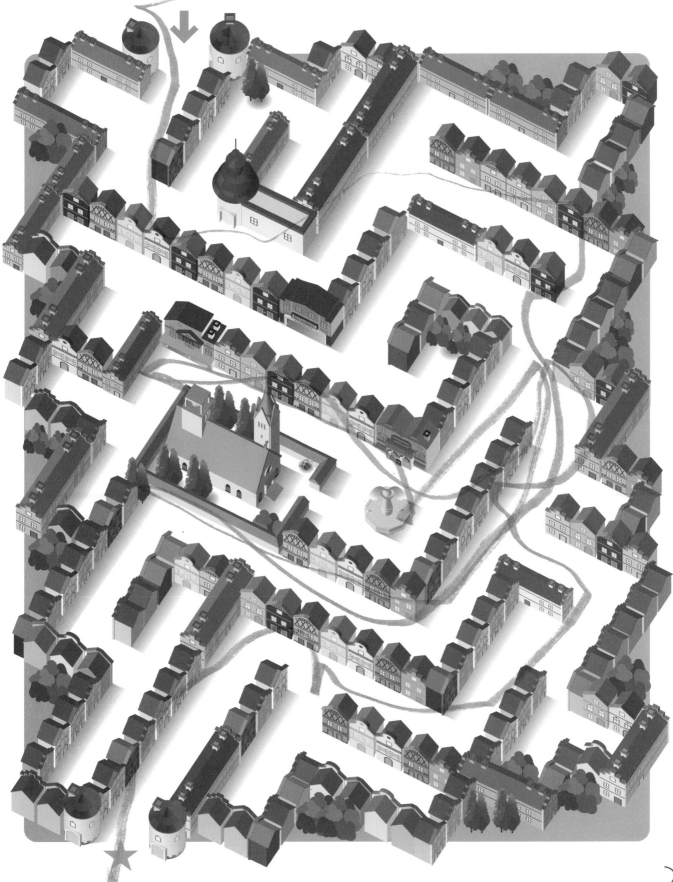

21

Draw a line from the arrow (➡)
to the star (★) by following the path.

Spring Lanes

Name
Gavin
Date
6-9-16

Draw a line from the arrow (→) to the star (★) by following the path.

Draw a line from the arrow (→) to the star (★) by following the path.

13 On the Farm

Name

Date

Draw a line from the arrow (→) to the star (★) by following the path.

25

Draw a line from the arrow (➡) to the star (★) by following the path.

Name

Date

Draw a line from the arrow (→) to the star (★) by following the path.

Draw a line from the arrow (→) to the star (★) by following the path.

Name

Date

Draw a line from the arrow (→) to the star (★) by following the path.

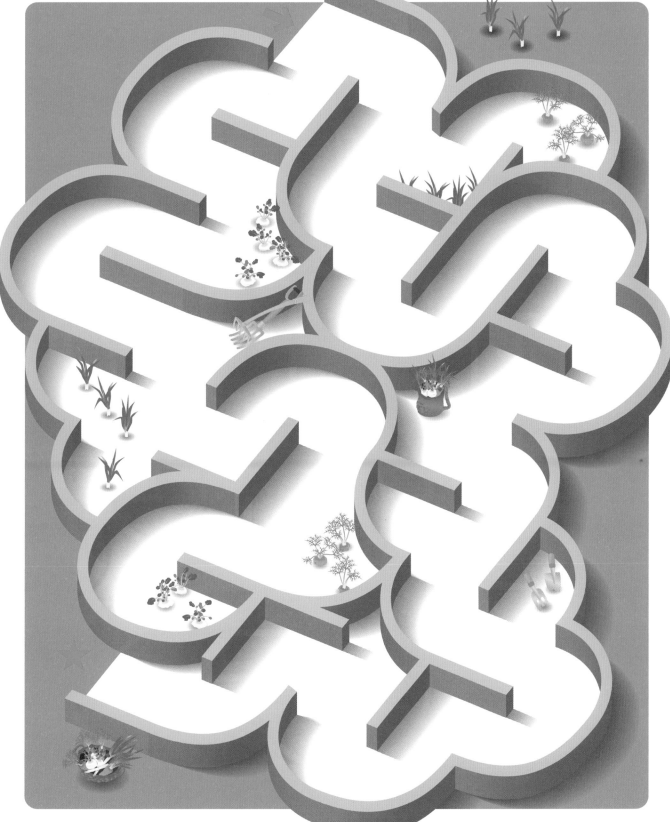

Draw a line from the arrow (➡) to the star (★) by following the path.

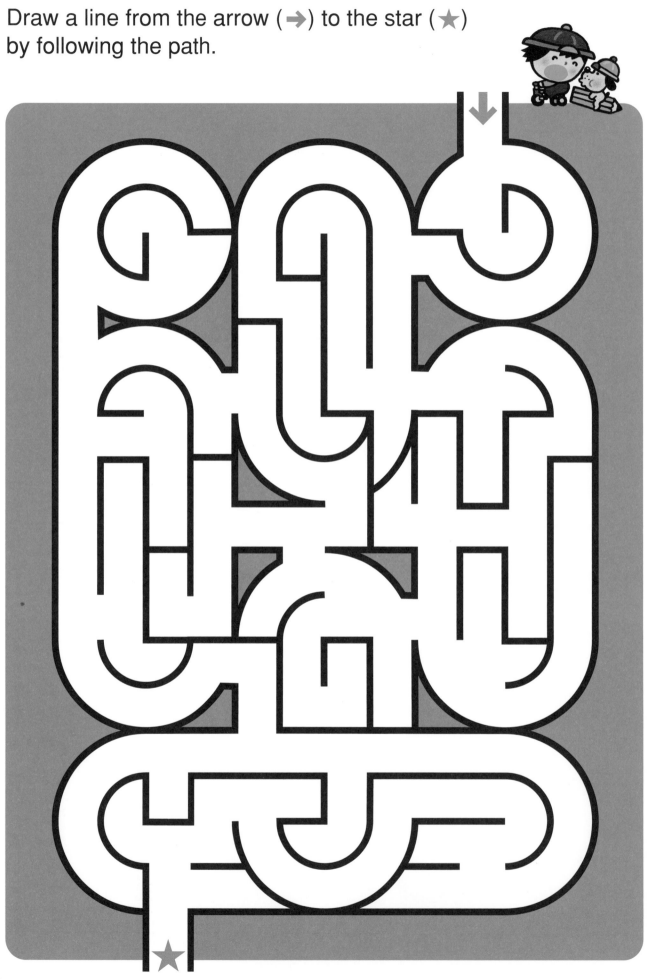

16 Through the Woods

Name

Date

Draw a line from the arrow (→) to the star (★) by following the path.

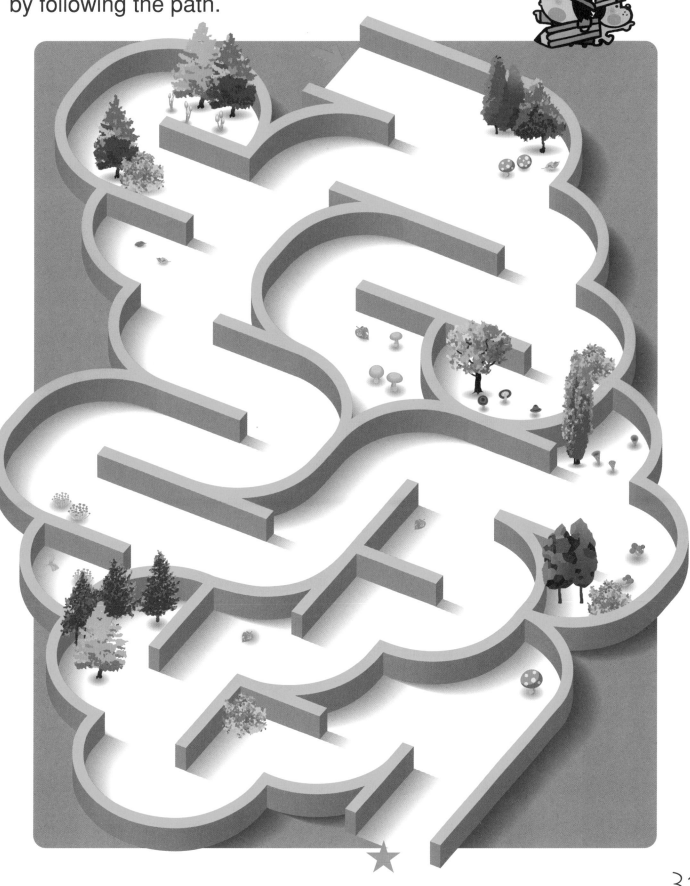

Draw a line from the arrow (→) to the star (★)
by following the path.

17 | Fish Bubbles and Crab Claws

Name

Date

Draw a line from the arrow (→) to the star (★) by following the path.

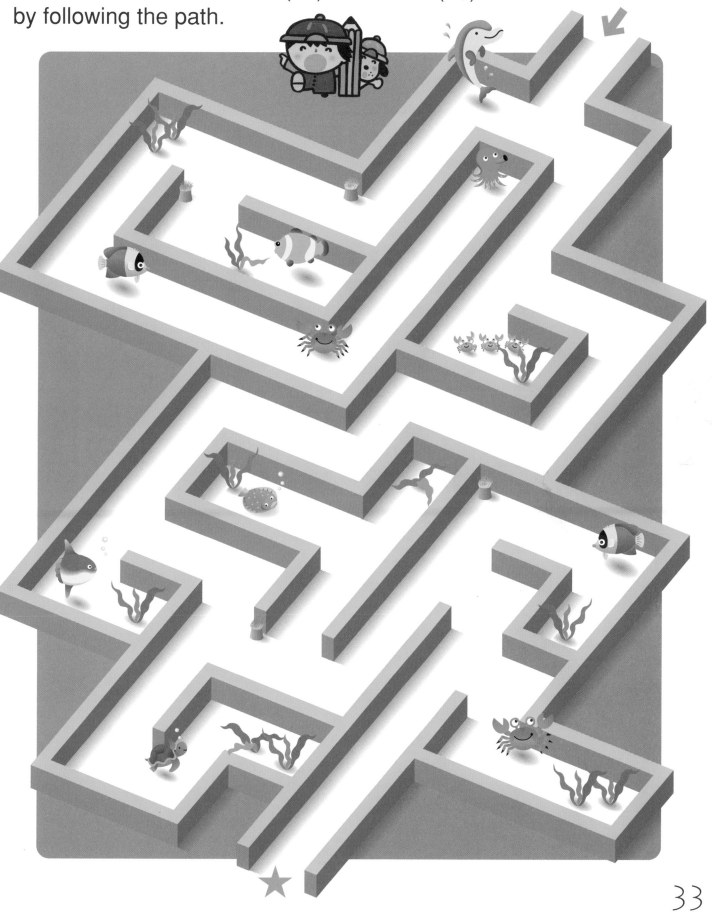

33

Draw a line from the arrow (➡) to the star (★) by following the path.

18 Looping Lanes

Draw a line from the arrow (➡) to the star (★) by following the path.

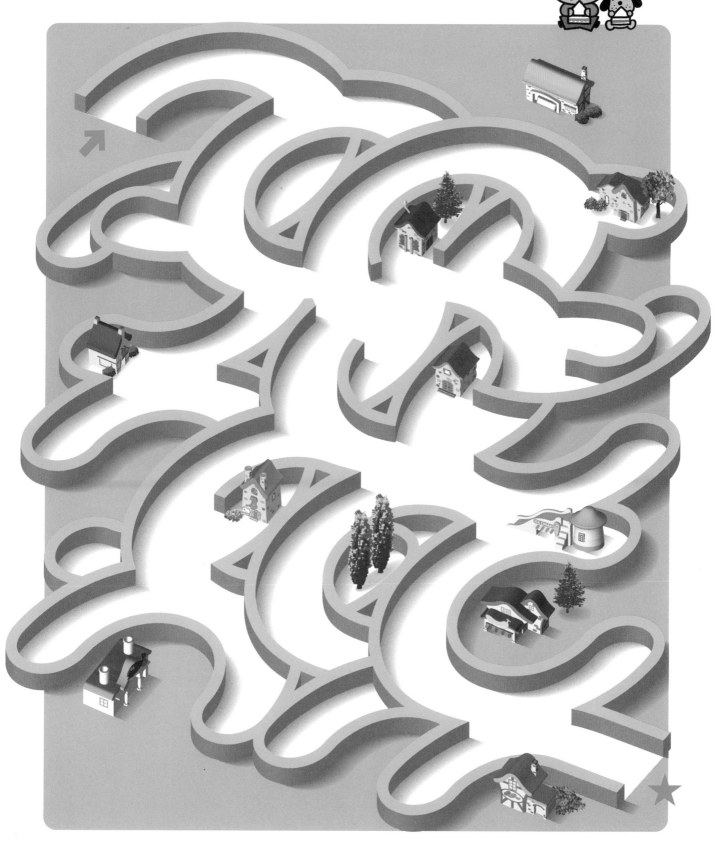

35

Draw a line from the arrow (➡) to the star (★)
by following the path.

19 Zoom Zoom 500

Name

Date

Draw a line from the arrow (➡) to the star (★)
by following the path.

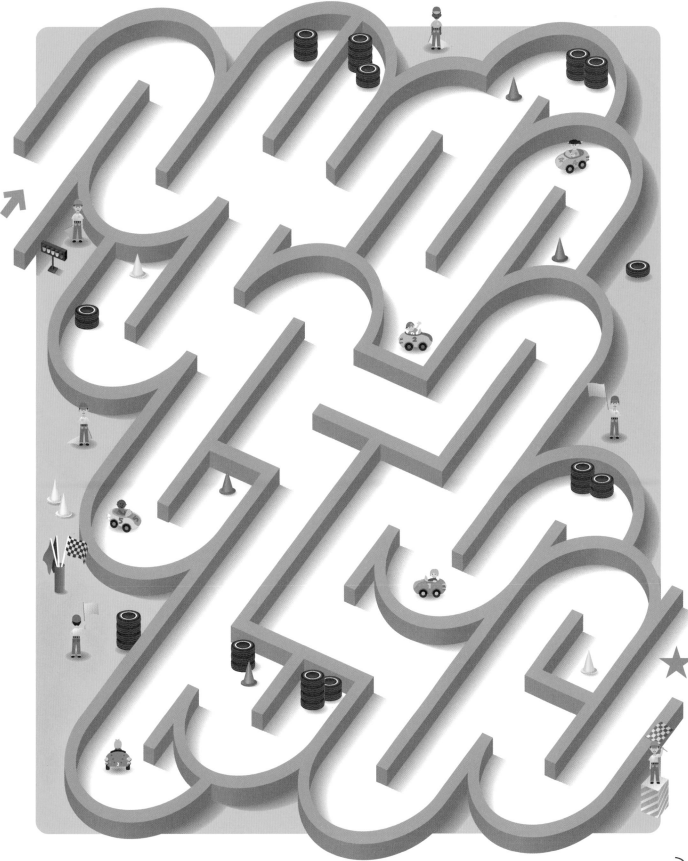

37

Draw a line from the arrow (➡) to the star (★) by following the path.

20 Autumn Lanes

Name

Date

Draw a line from the arrow (→) to the star (★) by following the path.

39

Draw a line from the arrow (→) to the star (★) by following the path.

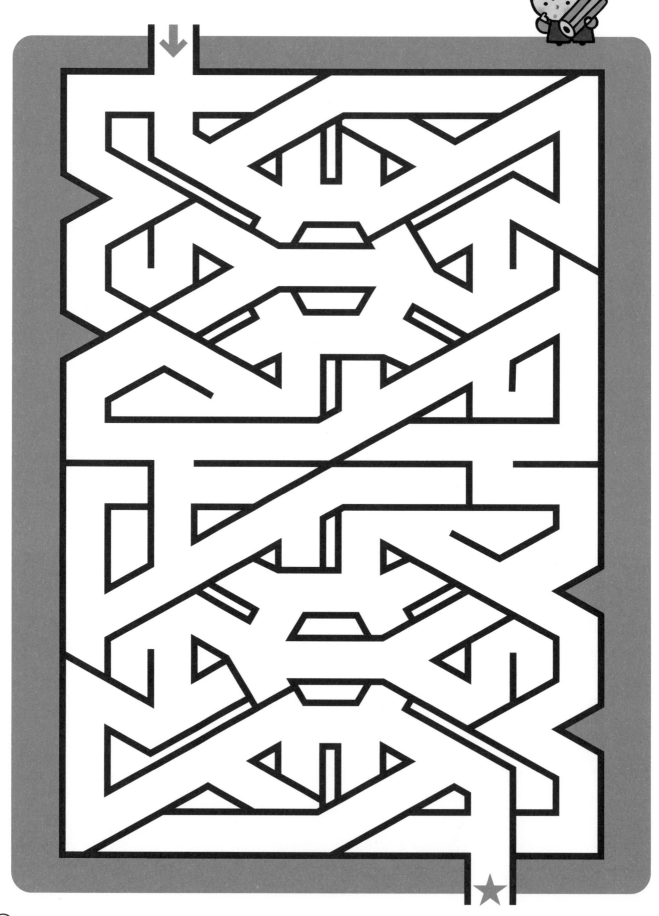

Palace Walk

Draw a line from the arrow (➜) to the star (★) by following the path.

Draw a line from the arrow (→) to the star (★) by following the path.

Garden Paths

Name

Date

Draw a line from the arrow (→) to the star (★) by following the path.

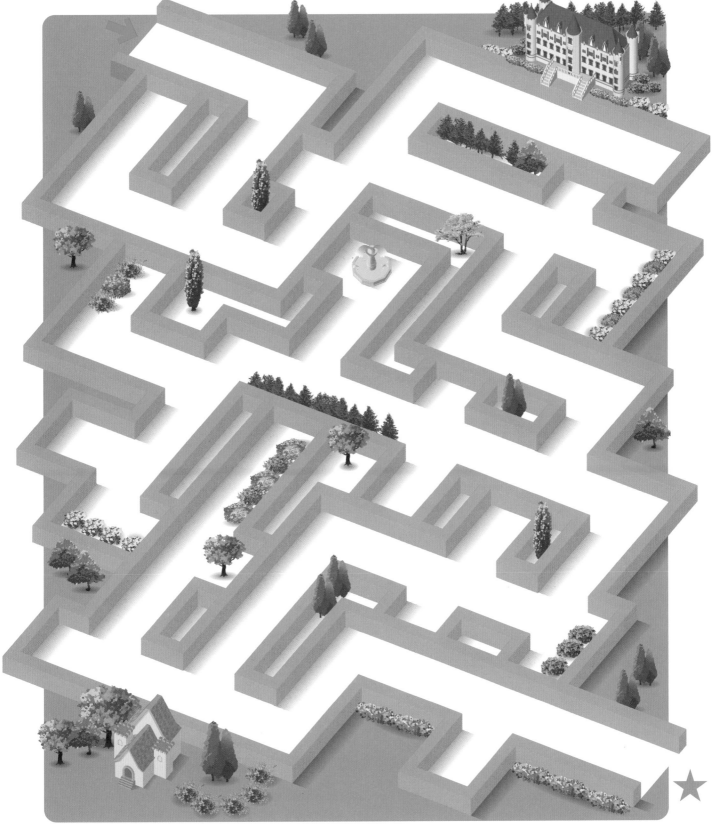

Draw a line from the arrow (→) to the star (★) by following the path.

23 Walking Tour

Name

Date

Draw a line from the arrow (→) to the star (★) by following the path.

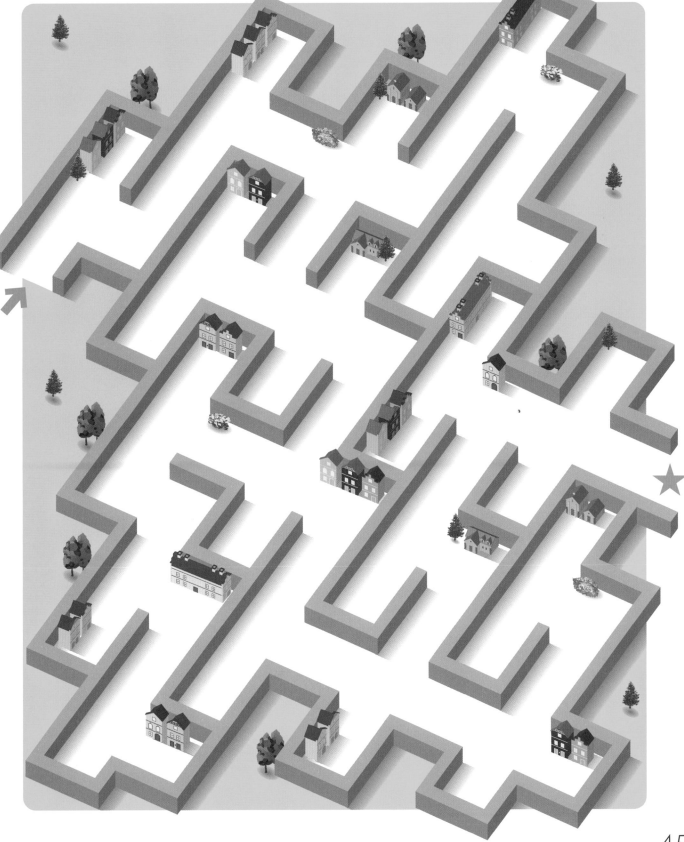

45

Draw a line from the arrow (➡) to the star (★)
by following the path.

24 | Prince's Pathways

Name

Date

Draw a line from the arrow (➡) to the star (★) by following the path.

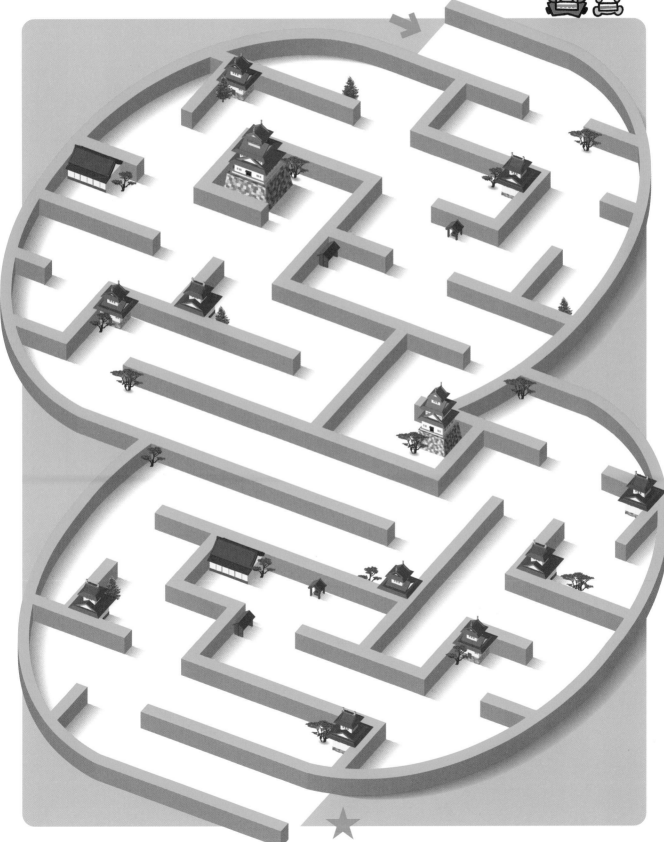

Draw a line from the arrow (→) to the star (★)
by following the path.

48

25 Wishing Well Farm

Draw a line from the arrow (→) to the star (★) by following the path.

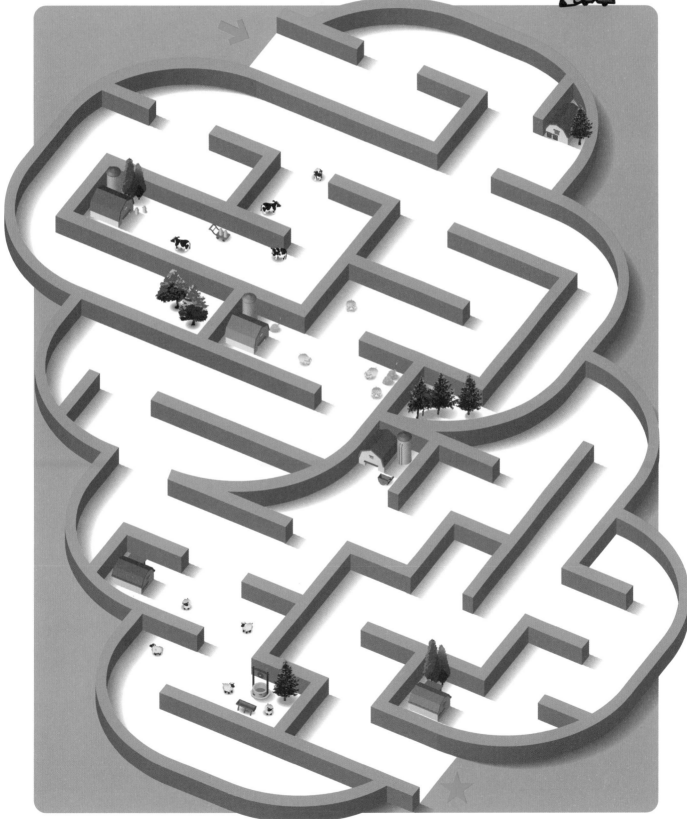

49

Draw a line from the arrow (→) to the star (★) by following the path.

Name

Date

Draw a line from the arrow (→) to the star (★) by following the path.

Draw a line from the arrow (→) to the star (★) by following the path.

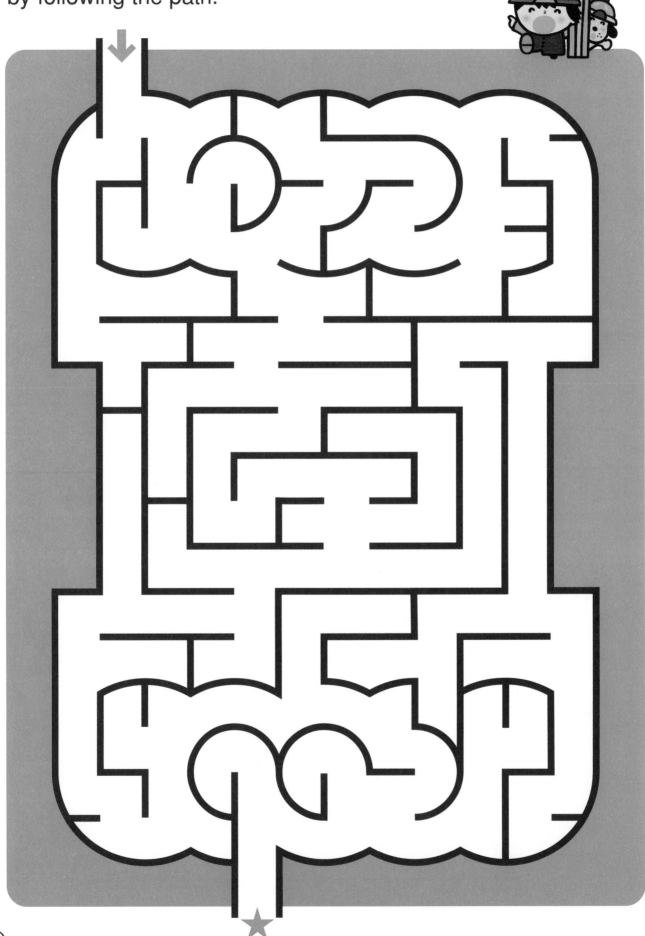

52

Gathering Garden Vegetables

Name

Date

Draw a line from the arrow (→) to the star (★) by following the path.

Draw a line from the arrow (→) to the star (★) by following the path.

54

28 Dinosaur Park

Name

Date

Draw a line from the arrow (➡) to the star (★)
by following the path.

Draw a line from the arrow (→) to the star (★) by following the path.

56

29 | Cook

Name

Date

To parents
Starting with this page, the maze patterns are different from others in the book. Mazes on even-numbered pages have narrower paths and are more challenging. When your child completes each exercise, praise him or her.

Draw a line from the arrow (→) to the star (★) by following the path.

57

Draw a line from the arrow (→)
to the star (★) by following the path.

58

Name

Date

Draw a line from the arrow (→) to the star (★) by following the path.

Draw a line from the arrow (→)
to the star (★) by following the path.

Name

Date

Draw a line from the arrow (➡) to the star (★) by following the path.

Draw a line from the arrow (→)
to the star (★) by following the path.

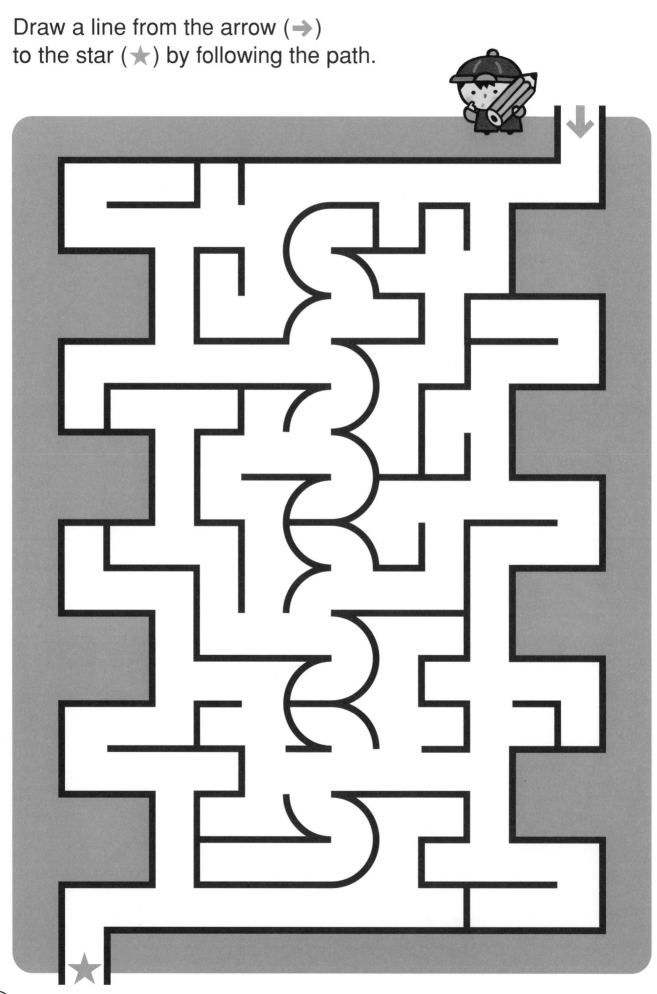

32 Firefighter

Draw a line from the arrow (→) to the star (★) by following the path.

63

Draw a line from the arrow (→) to the star (★) by following the path.

Name

Date

Draw a line from the arrow (➡) to the star (★) by following the path.

Draw a line from the arrow (➡) to the star (★)
by following the path.

Name

Date

Draw a line from the arrow (➡) to the star (★) by following the path.

Draw a line from the arrow (→)
to the star (★) by following the path.

Name

Date

Draw a line from the arrow (→) to the star (★) by following the path.

Draw a line from the arrow (➡) to the star (★) by following the path.

70

 **Doctor**

Draw a line from the arrow (→) to the star (★) by following the path.

Draw a line from the arrow (➡) to the star (★) by following the path.

72

 **Astronaut**

Name

Date

Draw a line from the arrow (➡) to the star (★) by following the path.

Draw a line from the arrow (→) to the star (★) by following the path.

Name

Date

Draw a line from the arrow (→) to the star (★) by following the path.

Draw a line from the arrow (→) to the star (★) by following the path.

 **Diver**

Name

Date

Draw a line from the arrow (➡) to the star (★) by following the path.

Challenge! ❶

To parents
The maze pattern on this page is different from others in the book.
Do the practice along with your child if he or she has difficulty.
Make sure that the line is vertical or horizontal, not diagonal.

Draw a line from the arrow (➡) to the star (★),
connecting only rabbit (🐰) to lion (🦁) or lion (🦁) to rabbit (🐰).

78

Name

Date

Draw a line from the arrow (➡) to the star (★) by following the path.

Challenge! ❷

To parents
The maze pattern on this page is different from others in the book.
Do the practice along with your child if he or she has difficulty.
Make sure that the line is vertical or horizontal, not diagonal.

Draw a line from the arrow (➡) to the star (★),
connecting only bear (🐻) to rabbit (🐰) or rabbit (🐰) to bear (🐻).

80

KUM☺N

Certificate of Achievement

is hereby congratulated on completing

Amazing Mazes

Presented on _____ , 20 _____

_____
Parent or Guardian